BIOLOGICAL WEAPONS

ALIX WOOD

PowerKiDS
press™

NEW YORK

Published in 2016 by **Rosen Publishing**
29 East 21st Street, New York, NY 10010

Cataloging-in-Publication Data
Wood, Alix.
Biological weapons / by Alix Wood.
p. cm. — (Today's high-tech weapons)
Includes index.
ISBN 978-1-5081-4671-1 (pbk.)
ISBN 978-1-5081-4672-8 (6-pack)
ISBN 978-1-5081-4673-5 (library binding)
1. Biological warfare — Juvenile literature. 2. Biological weapons —
Juvenile literature. I. Wood, Alix. II. Title.
UG447.8 W66 2016
358'.38—d23

Editor: Eloise Macgregor
Designer: Alix Wood
Consultant: Mark Baker

Photo Credits: Cover © Shutterstock/Eky Studio (top), © Shutterstock/
optimarc (ctr), © Shutterstock/BillionPhotos (btm); 4, 6, 7, 11, 12, 18,
21 top, 25, 26 © Dollar Photo Club; 8 © Edward S. Curtis; 9, 19 © CDC
Public Health Image Library; 13 © Hedwig Wachenheimer Epstein, 14 ©
UNMEER/Martine Perret; 15 bottom © National Cancer Institute; 16 ©
Masao Takezawa; 20 © Alamy; 21 bottom, 28 © DoD; 23 © Brad Collis;
24 © Shutterstock; 27 © US Navy/Joseph R. Schmitt; all other images are
in the public domain

Manufactured in the United States of America
CPSIA Compliance Information: Batch #BW16PK.
For Further Information contact Rosen Publishing, New York, New York at 1-800-237-9932

CONTENTS

WHAT ARE BIOLOGICAL WEAPONS?

Biological weapons use **toxins**, **bacteria**, and **viruses** to kill or harm humans, animals, or plants as an act of war. People have used biological weapons for thousands of years. In the Middle East 3,300 years ago, the Hittites from what is now Turkey sent infected livestock into enemy territory to infect their enemies with disease. During the Middle Ages in Britain, the corpses of people who died of **bubonic plague** were catapulted over castle walls as a form of biological attack!

In modern times, biological weapons (often called bioweapons) have become very high-tech.

BIOLOGICAL WEAPON FACT FILE:

WHO WOULD USE THE WEAPONS: Terrorists and the military could use bioweapons

CAUSE FOR CONCERN: An attack could cause millions of deaths

PROTECTION AGAINST BIOWAR: Antibiotics, vaccines, and good hygiene can protect against some types of bioweapons. Good training on how to react to a threat, and how to keep disease from spreading, is also vital.

ACCEPTABLE?: No. The use of biological weapons has been banned by international law since 1925.

The symbol in the warning triangle above is the international symbol for biological hazards. There are four levels of biohazard; level one has the least risk, and level four has the most extreme risk.

Biological weapons do not have to be able to kill people to help win a war. If a virus can kill crops or animals that people eat, the target country will have little food and become weak.

Bioweapons scientists have used infected insects to spread diseases to animals, crops, or humans.

SARIN ATTACK

On Monday, March 20, 1995, five members of the **religious cult** Aum Shinrikyo went down into Tokyo's subway, one of the world's busiest commuter transport systems, at morning rush hour. They each carried bags of liquid sarin wrapped in newspaper, and an umbrella with a sharpened tip. Each man boarded a different train. At prearranged stations, they dropped the sarin packets, punctured them with the tips of their umbrellas, and then got off the train.

Sarin poisoning is very rare. Many Tokyo hospitals only knew how to treat patients because a professor at Shinshu University's school of medicine saw reports on television. Dr. Nobuo Yanagisawa recognized the symptoms, and sent information on treatment to hospitals in Tokyo by fax!

The Tokyo subway attack killed 12 people, severely injured 50 more, and caused temporary eye problems for around 1,000 others.

The United Nations Security Council have classified sarin as a **weapon of mass destruction**. Sarin attacks the nervous system and is 26 times more deadly than cyanide poison. A person's clothing can release sarin for around 30 minutes after contact with the gas, so anyone treating a patient must also protect themselves.

SARIN FACT FILE:

TYPE: Nerve agent

APPEARANCE: Colorless, odorless gas

STRENGTH: A 0.5 milligram dose can kill a person in one minute

SPECIAL INFORMATION: Sarin is liquid at room temperature but then turns into a gas, allowing it to spread quickly

TREATMENT: The drug, atropine, can help if injected right away. The skin and eyes must be washed thoroughly.

DEADLY SMALLPOX

Smallpox is a deadly disease caused by a virus. The World Health Organization believes that around 15 million people caught the disease and two million people died from it in the year 1967, alone. After a ten-year program **vaccinating** people against the disease, smallpox was wiped out. However, in some government science laboratories around the world, scientists stored copies of the disease to use as a bioweapon.

Smallpox was used in one of the world's first biological attacks. In 1763, Sir Jeffrey Amherst, commander of the British Forces in Ottawa, Canada, is believed to have given smallpox-infected blankets to Native American tribes. The tribes had no immunity to the disease and many died.

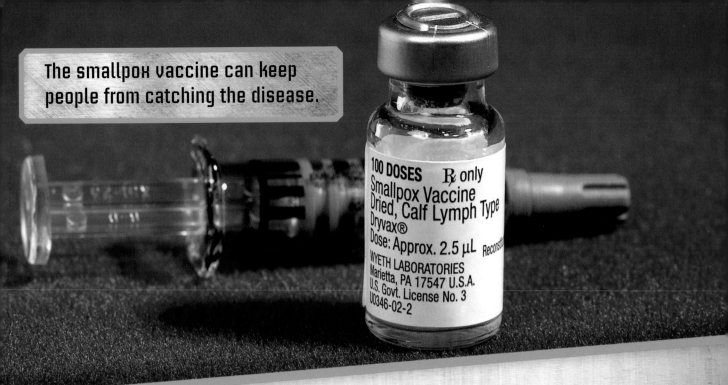

The smallpox vaccine can keep people from catching the disease.

100 DOSES ℞ only
Smallpox Vaccine
Dried, Calf Lymph Type
Dryvax®
Dose: Approx. 2.5 µL Reconstit...
WYETH LABORATORIES
Marietta, PA 17547 U.S.A.
U.S. Govt. License No. 3
U0346-02-2

SMALLPOX FACT FILE:

TYPE: Virus

HOW DOES IT SPREAD?: Person to person

SYMPTOMS: High temperature, headaches and backache, pink bumps on the skin

HOW DEADLY IS IT?: Around one third of people who catch smallpox die from it

TREATMENT: A very effective vaccine is available which has successfully wiped out smallpox in the past

In 1989, a senior Soviet scientist admitted that the Soviet Union had a large smallpox bioweapons program. They had designed a way to spread the disease using bombs and missiles. Smallpox was now more dangerous than it had been years ago because people were no longer being vaccinated against it.

Because a vaccine exists, however, countries could protect people if they thought a threat was likely.

ANTHRAX LETTERS

In September 2001, seven days after the terrorist attacks on the World Trade Center and the Pentagon, the U.S. was on high alert. Letters containing anthrax **spores** began arriving on the desks of news offices in New York City and Boca Raton, Florida. The letters had a Trenton, New Jersey, postmark. The letters' first victim, Robert Stevens, went to a Florida hospital feeling unwell and short of breath. He died four days later.

SPECIAL REWARD
Up to $2.5 million

For information leading to the arrest and conviction of the individual(s) responsible for the mailing of letters containing anthrax to the New York Post, Tom Brokaw at NBC, Senator Tom Daschle and Senator Patrick Leahy:

AS A RESULT OF EXPOSURE TO ANTHRAX, FIVE (5) PEOPLE HAVE DIED.

The person responsible for these deaths...
- Likely has a scientific background/work history which may include a specific familiarity with anthrax
- Has a level of comfort in and around the Trenton, NJ area due to present or prior association

Anyone having information, contact **America's Most Wanted** at **1-800-CRIME TV** or the **FBI** via e-mail at **amerithrax@fbi.gov**

All information will be held in strict confidence. Reward payment will be made in accordance with the conditions of Postal Service Reward Poster 296, dated February 2000. Source of reward funds: U.S. Postal Service and FBI $2,000,000; ADVO, Inc. $500,000.

Three weeks after the news offices' letters, two more letters were sent to Democratic senators in Washington, D.C. In all, the anthrax letters killed five people and infected 17 others with the disease.

The FBI investigating the poisonings began to suspect that the culprit was an American scientist who worked at a government biodefense laboratory in Maryland. The suspect died from an **overdose** in 2008. His guilt has never been proven.

Dozens of buildings were contaminated with anthrax as a result of the mailings. The cleanup of the postal facilities and government buildings took many months and is believed to have cost over $1 billion!

ANTHRAX FACT FILE:

TYPE: Bacteria

HOW DOES IT SPREAD?: By touching, inhaling, or eating the spores

SYMPTOMS: High temperature, breathing problems, tiredness, black **ulcers**

HOW DEADLY IS IT?: Once inhaled it is deadly. A few people have survived after immediate medical treatment.

SPECIAL INFORMATION: Anthrax has a long shelf life. It is still deadly even after 40 or more years.

TREATMENT : There is an effective vaccine and antibiotics can treat it

Anthrax bacteria live in soil, so grazing animals can easily become infected.

NAZI BIOWEAPONS

The Nazi Party was a political group that ruled Germany between 1933 and 1945. During World War II, their biological warfare program carried out deadly experiments on 1,700 prisoners in **concentration camps**. Killer diseases such as plague, typhoid, cholera, and anthrax were developed into weapons.

The Germans also forced prisoners to produce chemical weapons. Prisoners filled bombs and shells with the dangerous nerve agent, tabun. Fortunately the factory was taken by the Soviet army before the Germans were able to use the weapons.

CHOLERA FACT FILE:

TYPE: Bacteria

SYMPTOMS: Upset stomach, vomiting and leg cramps

STRENGTH: If the bacteria enters the water supply, the disease spreads rapidly

TREATMENT : Antibiotics, fluids, and zinc

The German prisoner of war camp, Auschwitz

The Nazi Party employed some of the best scientists to help them develop bioweapons. Before the war, Kurt Blome was an important German scientist. During World War II he was ordered to experiment with plague vaccines on concentration camp prisoners. There was also evidence that Blome experimented with sarin gas on prisoners in Auschwitz.

Erich Traub was a German veterinarian and scientist. He worked on the deadly virus foot-and-mouth, which is believed to have been used on cattle and reindeer in Russia.

Kurt Blome

Although Traub and Blome were war criminals, they were brought to the United States in 1949. Operation Paperclip was a U.S. program in which over 1,500 German scientists, technicians, and engineers from Nazi Germany and other countries were brought to the United States after World War II, so that their scientific knowledge could be used, and to keep it from being used by the Soviet Union.

THE THREAT OF EBOLA

Despite being a relatively new disease, the word "Ebola" strikes fear in the heart of people who have seen its effects in West Africa. Ebola is classified as a level 4 biohazard, which is the most dangerous. When the disease first appeared, some countries suspected that Ebola had been created specially for use as a bioweapon. The North Korean media suggested it had been created and spread by the U.S. military. Governments are often suspicious when a new disease suddenly appears. It is now generally believed that the disease was spread naturally by infected fruit bats.

Medical teams must wear protective clothing when treating Ebola patients.

EBOLA FACT FILE:

TYPE: Virus

HOW DOES IT SPREAD?: Contact with infected bodily fluid, such as blood

SYMPTOMS: Fever, sore throat, pain and headaches, then sickness and a rash

HOW DEADLY IS IT?: 50 percent of people who catch Ebola will die from the disease

TREATMENT: There is no known cure, but treatment can help someone survive

The Ebola virus under a microscope

Could Ebola be made into a weapon of mass destruction? It seems unlikely. The virus doesn't spread quickly. A person sick with Ebola will usually only infect around two more people. However, experts believe there is a risk of a small-scale attack. The virus could be put in a small bomb. An explosion could infect a few hundred people if the virus was inhaled, or infected open cuts.

At present there is no vaccine or effective treatment of the virus. Scientists around the world are racing to try to find a cure, as thousands of people suffer from a recent large outbreak in West Africa.

PLAGUE BOMBS

During World War II, Japanese planes flew over two cities in China and dropped the most unusual bombs. Sacks containing disease-infected fleas, rats, and rags were dropped onto the cities of Ningbo and Quzhou.

The bubonic plague-carrying fleas caused a serious outbreak of the disease. At least 109 people died in Ningbo, in just two months. Residents fled Quzhou after the attack there, unfortunately helping spread the disease to surrounding areas. Quzhou had never suffered from bubonic plague before. Around 50,000 people died from the disease in the years following the attack.

General Shirō Ishii ran the Japanese biological warfare project at Unit 731.

PLAGUE FACT FILE:

TYPE: Bacteria

STRENGTH: If untreated, bubonic plague kills around 50 percent of people infected

SYMPTOMS: Swellings found under the arm and around the neck and groin, fever and cramps

TREATMENT: Antibiotics within 24 hours of the first symptoms

One of the Unit 731 buildings, near Harbin, China, where Japan's secret biological weapons were made

Japan's biological warfare program employed some of Japan's top doctors and scientists. A huge compound of around 150 buildings was built in 1936 near Harbin in north China, which was then under Japanese control.

Their work was top secret. Everyone was told that the scientists were working on water purification. Scientists at Unit 731 experimented on Chinese civilians and prisoners of war. They tested biological weapons and the methods of delivering them, such as by firearm and by bomb.

During the last months of World War II, Japan planned to use bubonic plague as a biological weapon on the people of San Diego, California. The attack was scheduled to happen on September 22, 1945. Fortunately, Japan surrendered just five weeks earlier.

KILLER BUNNIES

Can cute, fluffy rabbits really be bioweapons manufacturers? The answer is "yes." Tularemia is a disease spread by rabbits, hares, and rodents. Humans catch the disease after contact with infected animals, by eating them, or being bitten by infected insects that live on the animals. Tularemia has been made into a very effective biological weapon.

Kenneth Alibek, a former Soviet biological weapons scientist, blames a 1942 outbreak of tularemia on deliberate biological warfare. Thousands of German soldiers at the siege of Stalingrad became ill. The disease is believed to have been released by the Soviet forces.

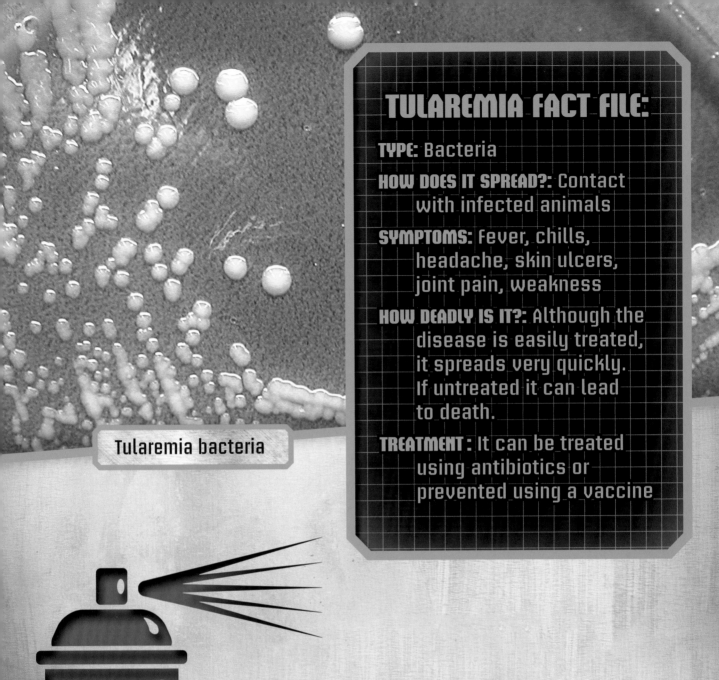

TULAREMIA FACT FILE:

TYPE: Bacteria

HOW DOES IT SPREAD?: Contact with infected animals

SYMPTOMS: Fever, chills, headache, skin ulcers, joint pain, weakness

HOW DEADLY IS IT?: Although the disease is easily treated, it spreads very quickly. If untreated it can lead to death.

TREATMENT : It can be treated using antibiotics or prevented using a vaccine

Tularemia bacteria

A rabbit is not a very effective biological weapon. But biological weapons scientists have taken the tularemia bacteria and created a version that can be sprayed by aerosol. This method of spreading the disease creates the most serious form of tularemia. Symptoms include cough, chest pain, and difficulty breathing.

FORT DETRICK

Fort Detrick, Maryland, was the center of the U.S. biological weapons program from 1943 to 1969. When the U.S. decided to stop producing bioweapons, Fort Detrick became the center for the U.S. biological defense program. Scientists and military personnel work on ways to defend against biological attack.

The U.S. Army Medical Research Institute of Infectious Diseases (USAMRIID) helped the FBI investigate the 2001 anthrax letter attacks (see pages 10-11). USAMRIID eventually became the focus of the FBI's investigation, too, as one of the chief suspects worked at the center! The type of anthrax used in the attacks was held at USAMRIID. It has never been proven that the worker was the culprit, however.

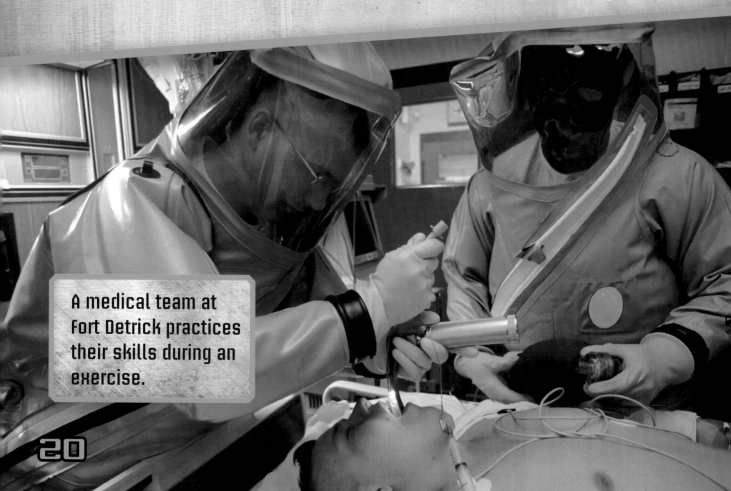

A medical team at Fort Detrick practices their skills during an exercise.

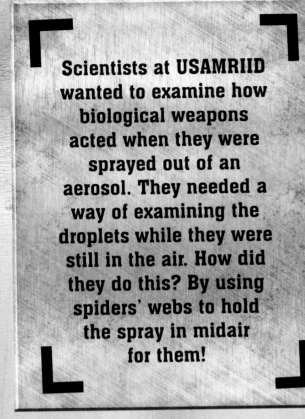

Scientists at USAMRIID wanted to examine how biological weapons acted when they were sprayed out of an aerosol. They needed a way of examining the droplets while they were still in the air. How did they do this? By using spiders' webs to hold the spray in midair for them!

During times of war, USAMRIID provides the military with advice, vaccines, and medicine to protect soldiers against biological attacks. USAMRIID scientists also train and equip special laboratory teams so that they are able to identify any dangerous biological weapons while in a war zone.

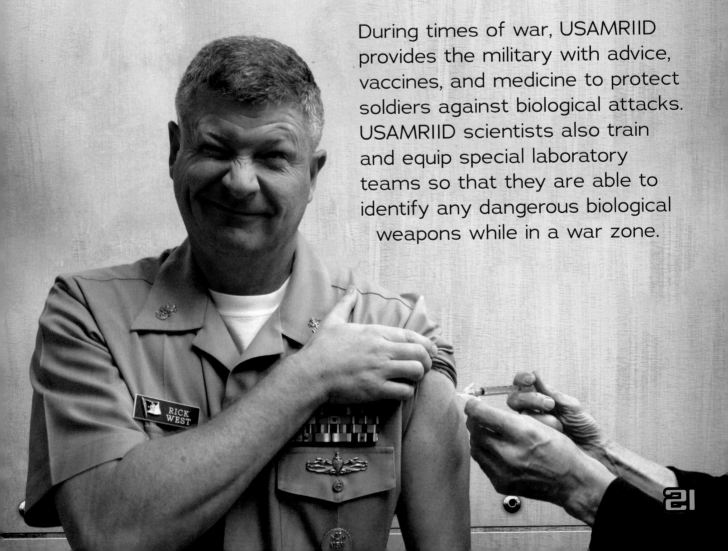

RICE BLAST

Biological weapons aren't just aimed at infecting people. Rice blast harms food crops. Lack of food can have a big effect on a country's ability to fight a war. Rice blast is a disease that affects rice crops. In countries where rice is a main food source, the disease could cause people to starve, and keep people from earning money from their crops.

A number of countries, including the U.S., have looked at using rice blast as a possible biological weapon. The U.S. anticrop program developed during the 1950s and 1960s had made nearly a ton of rice blast by the time the program was ended. The disease would have been used for an attack on Asia, where rice is a major crop.

Women in Cambodia planting rice

The U.S. army tested rice blast in Okinawa, Japan, and in the Midwest of the U.S. in the early 1960s. They released rice blast fungus over rice crops to study what happened to the crop. Rice blast has been listed as a significant biological weapon by the Centers for Disease Control and Prevention. Experts believe each year enough rice to feed 60 million people is destroyed by rice blast disease!

RICE BLAST FACT FILE:

TYPE: Fungus

HOW DOES IT SPREAD?: By wind-borne spores, by water, and by contact with infected plant material

SYMPTOMS: Gray-white marks on the leaves. The fungus may also attack the stem of the plant.

HOW DEADLY IS IT?: It spreads very rapidly and severely affects the rice crop

RINDERPEST

When the Mongol leader, Genghis Khan, invaded Europe in the 13th century, his cattle accidentally spread a disease. Known as rinderpest, the deadly virus can infect cattle, goats, bison, and giraffe. Genghis Khan spread the disease by accident, but in modern warfare, countries such as the U.K., Canada, and the U.S. have considered spreading the disease on purpose as a bioweapon.

Spreading a disease that affects livestock harms an enemy in a similar way as spreading a disease that affects crops. People rely on the animals as a source of food. Also, wild animals, such as lions, may turn to humans as a food source if their usual prey has died out.

A statue of Genghis Khan

A diseased herd can ruin a farmer's livelihood.

People cannot catch rinderpest, and most experts say that people suffer no harm from eating infected meat. However, once the cattle have all died out, the food supply disappears. The money that farmers made by selling their animals disappears, too, harming the country's wealth.

RINDERPEST FACT FILE:

TYPE: Virus

HOW DOES IT SPREAD?: The disease spreads very rapidly, usually by direct contact with an infected animal. The disease can spread through infected animal feed and water, also.

HOW DEADLY IS IT?: An infected animal usually dies 5 -10 days after first becoming ill

TREATMENT: Any animal suspected of having the disease should be separated from others. A vaccine can prevent the disease.

CHIMERA

In ancient mythology, a chimera was a creature made from a mixture of a lion, a goat, and a serpent. The creature became a symbol of evil. In biological warfare, a chimera is a **genetically engineered** virus. Not all chimera are evil. Some can create cures for illnesses, for example the common cold virus mixed with the polio virus is believed to help cure brain cancer.

Some bioweapons experts are using the idea of a chimera virus to create truly lethal weapons. Scientists have discovered ways to create viruses that could trigger two diseases at once. It is believed that during the 1980s in the Soviet Union, scientists studied the possibility of combining smallpox and Ebola.

In the future, bioweapons scientists could create "stealth viruses." These viruses remain harmless until activated by a **trigger**. Possible triggers could include being treated with the vaccine that prevents the chosen stealth virus. If a vaccine caused the disease it was supposed to prevent, people would start to lose trust in their government. Mistrust can help an enemy win a war, too.

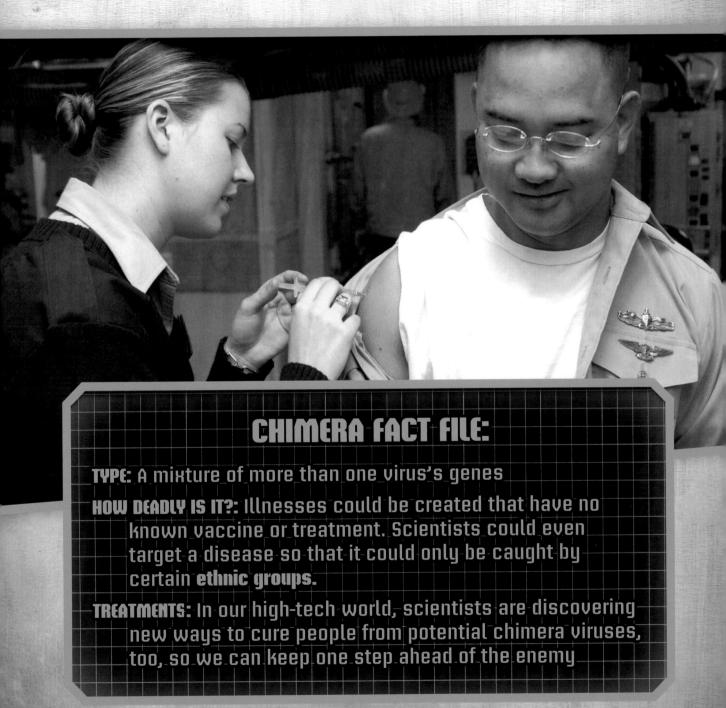

CHIMERA FACT FILE:

TYPE: A mixture of more than one virus's genes

HOW DEADLY IS IT?: Illnesses could be created that have no known vaccine or treatment. Scientists could even target a disease so that it could only be caught by certain **ethnic groups.**

TREATMENTS: In our high-tech world, scientists are discovering new ways to cure people from potential chimera viruses, too, so we can keep one step ahead of the enemy

DEFENSE AGAINST BIOWEAPONS

There are several high-tech ways that a country can protect itself against biological weapons. Scientists are developing devices that can detect toxins using tiny electronic chips containing living nerve cells. Plants are also being developed that change color in the event of a biological attack.

A **hazmat** suit protects people against hazardous materials such as biological agents. The suits often have breathing apparatus. To help prevent any biological agents entering the suit the seams are sealed with tape. Working in a hazmat suit is hard. The suits can be stiff and very hot to wear.

A hazmat suit and breathing apparatus

Hazmat teams need to clean up after a biological attack. Clothing can spread a virus or toxin unless thoroughly cleaned. **Decontamination** is usually done by scrubbing using warm soapy water or a mixture of water and bleach. Talcum powder or flour can be used to soak up liquid agents. Once the liquid is absorbed, the powder is brushed off. As fast as people develop deadly weapons, you can be sure that people are thinking up ways to protect us from them.

Biological attacks are hard to detect. Experts look out for suspicious signs such as dead or dying animals, unexplained odors, low-lying clouds of dust, or oily droplets on surfaces. They also look out for suspicious people, such as people wearing long sleeves in hot weather, or wearing breathing protection.

A hazmat team practices decontamination.

GLOSSARY

antibiotics: Substances that kill bacteria.

bacteria: Microorganisms that can cause disease.

bubonic plague: An infectious disease causing chills, fever, weakness, and swellings.

concentration camps: Places for confining political prisoners and enemies of a nation.

decontamination: The process of cleansing to remove hazardous materials.

ethnic groups: People of the same race or nationality.

fungus: A spore-producing organism, including mold, yeast, and mushrooms.

genetically engineered: When genes in an organism are deliberately manipulated.

hazmat: Short for "hazardous materials."

microscope: An instrument used to see very small things.

nerve agent: A dangerous chemical agent that interferes with nerve impulses.

overdose: An excessive and dangerous dose of a drug.

religious cult: A small religious group regarded as extreme or dangerous.

spores: Tiny cells produced by nonflowering plants and bacteria.

terrorists: People or groups that scare or threaten with violence illegally.

toxins: Poisons made by a plant or an animal that harm another plant or animal.

trigger: Something that causes a device to function.

ulcers: Open sores.

vaccinating: Treating with a vaccine to produce immunity against a disease.

vaccines: Injections that keep a person from getting a disease.

viruses: A small living thing that causes a disease.

weapon of mass destruction: A weapon that can kill or harm a large number of humans or cause great damage.

FOR MORE INFORMATION

BOOKS

Barnard, Bryn. *Outbreak! Plagues That Changed History*. New York, NY: Crown Books for Young Readers, 2005.

Friedlander, Mark P., Jr. *Outbreak: Disease Detectives at Work* (Discovery!). Minneapolis, MN: Twenty First Century Books, 2009.

Nardo, Don. *Invisible Weapons: The Science of Biological and Chemical Warfare* (Headline Science). North Mankato, MN: Compass Point Books, 2010.

Walker, Richard. *Epidemics and Plagues* (Kingfisher Knowledge). London: Kingfisher Books Ltd, 2009.

Due to the changing nature of Internet links, PowerKids Press has developed an online list of websites related to the subject of this book. This site is updated regularly. Please use this link to access the list:
www.powerkidslinks.com/thtw/bio

INDEX